C000109201

Naxos - Tinos - Syros
Three Gems
of the Cyclades

Denis Roubien

Copyright © 2020 Denis Roubien
All rights reserved
ISBN: 9798669563479

This book is dedicated to the chief of our hiking group
and to my Naxian friend,
who made me discover some treasure islands

Contents

Naxos
From the precursor
of the Parthenon
to the Crusaders

Tinos
The last jewel
in the crown of Venice

Syros
The noble heart
of the Cyclades

Preface

I first visited the islands of Naxos, Tinos, and Syros as a child, accompanying my parents. At the time, but also for many years to come, these islands were a terra incognita. Only recently did they acquire, still relatively few, visitors who go beyond the obvious (the beaches) and discover a wealth of treasures in one of the culturally richest parts of Greece. I had the chance to be among these privileged few, first thanks to Nikos Gavalas, a local friend, and a little later thanks to Kostas Zarokostas, the chief of the hiking group in which I participate. This little book's purpose is to offer you a glimpse of this wealth and induce you to discover it for yourself. If you decide to do it, you will not be disappointed. The order of presentation of the islands was defined by the chronological order of their main monuments.

Naxos
From the precursor
of the Parthenon
to the Crusaders

Part I. The castle of Naxos
Time travel to the Duchy
of the Archipelago

1. Naxos becomes the seat of the crusaders

Wondering how Greece was under the domination of the crusaders? It seems to be something lost in the oblivion of the past and we will never get any idea of how it was? Perhaps you have not been in the right place. In Naxos, the less known part of Greek history exists and is alive like nowhere else.

During our hiking tour in Naxos, always under the guidance of Kostas, we found ourselves in the Castle of Chora (the capital). It is one of the best-preserved castles of the Aegean. And one of the few inhabited until today. This further increases its value. Which, anyway, is particularly great. Because this small piece of Naxos encapsulates a disproportionately important history.

In 1207, three years after the crusaders of the Fourth Crusade conquered the Byzantine Empire, Marco Sanudo, a Venetian nobleman, the nephew of the doge Enrico Dandolo, occupied most of the islands of the Cyclades. He founded the Duchy of the Archipelago and settled in Naxos.

2. A castle that stands out

photo by Denis Roubien

photo by Denis Roubien

The tower of Glezos, the only one of the five towers of the Castle still preserved

Most medieval settlements of the Aegean have a makeshift fortification. Namely, the inhabitants built their houses close to each other, leaving the exterior walls blind. So, they formed a wall that protected them from the greatest scourge of the Aegean for centuries: the pirates.

However, Naxos was not a random settlement. It was the seat of the Duke. Here lived the leader of the Cyclades and the Venetian noblemen who accompanied him to the conquest of the islands. Therefore, here security requirements were greater. Therefore, they built a regular wall, with five towers at the corners. Today, only one is preserved, the tower of Glezos.

Inside, in the centre, they built the two centres of power, as in all medieval cities of Western Europe: the centre of political power, namely, the palace of the Duke; and the centre of religious authority, namely, the catholic cathedral. Should enemies manage to get inside the walls, there was also the last refuge: the defensive tower. There the inhabitants would give the battle to the end. Today it is in ruins, but it is still impressive.

About the palace of Sanudo scholars disagree. Others say it's the half-ruined defensive tower. Others that it was a separate building, the one now housing the Catholic Archdiocese.

The defensive tower. Last refuge if the enemies came through the walls

The Catholic Archdiocese. It is said it was once the palace of Marco Sanudo

The Castle entrance from Pradouna Square

The Castle had three gates. We walked in through the most important, the Great Door (Trani Porta). On the pilaster, we saw engraved the Venetian cubit. When the draper came, the noblewomen of the Castle came to meet him at the Great Door. Thus, they used the engraved cubit to measure the fabrics they bought.

The Great Door (Trani Porta)

3. At the Metropolis of all Aegean

First, we entered the church of Candlemas. It is the Catholic cathedral of Naxos and seat of the Archbishop of Naxos and Tinos. He holds also the title of Metropolitan of all Aegean. The title is not random and reflects the island's history and the importance it had throughout the Aegean in the Middle Ages. Sanudo built the cathedral in the 13th century, but its present form dates from the 17th century.

photo by Denis Roubien

The Catholic cathedral of Candlemas

The top of the steeple of the Catholic cathedral is the highest point in Naxos Town

In the centre of the sanctuary, there is the icon of the Virgin of Mercy. It is one of the oldest in Greece and perhaps the only one that presents the full-length Virgin Mary holding Jesus Christ. Archaeologists date it back to the 11th-12th century. It's two-sided and on the backside, there is an image of John the Baptist. The icon has always been in that place but covered by a newer layer and with silver on top, to the feet of Jesus Christ. Thanks to the insistence of the then vicar, Father Emmanuel Remoundos, and the teamwork of conservators from the Byzantine Museum of Athens the old icon was discovered in 1970. They placed it in a rotating frame so that also the back image could be visible.

Catholic cathedral of Candlemas. The interior

Catholic cathedral of Candlemas. The Virgin of Mercy, one of the oldest icons in Greece

Afterwards, it was the turn of the Cappella Casazza, dedicated to the Immaculate Conception. It is said that it was the palace chapel of Sanudo. What is certain is that later it was the church of the Jesuit monastery. It is there that Father Emmanuel Remoundos, now former vicar, guides us. He tells us that the chapel is adjacent to the former Jesuit monastery, with which it communicates internally. He also reveals to us that it sits on the edge of the Castle, so its external side is in the air. Actually, the floor we step on has a huge gap underneath. He even shows us a drawing he made himself. It looks like a miniature of Mont Saint Michel in Normandy. What we think is the ground floor, is actually several floors above the ground.

Of course, we could not see this from within. Nevertheless, what we could see was a richly decorated baroque pulpit and respective altars with paintings of rare artistic value. And, as Father Emmanuel demonstrates to us, this space has excellent acoustics. In addition, another rare element is the Gothic cross vault with ribs above the sanctuary. In other countries, these things are common, but in Greece, they are very rare.

Next to the building of the Catholic Archdiocese, we visited the Virgin Mary Theoskepasti (Covered by God), the only Orthodox church in the Castle. Some say that it was already there when the Venetians arrived. Others, that Sanudo built it for his wife, who was Orthodox.

Cappella Casazza

The Gothic cross vault of the sanctuary of the Cappella Casazza

4. Schools of international fame

The huge complex of the convent of the Ursulines

The most impressive building in the Castle, however, is the convent of the Ursulines, which housed one of the most famous schools in the Eastern Mediterranean. Three schools operated in the Castle in respective monasteries. A girls' school in the convent of the Ursulines and two for boys. One in the monastery of the Capuchins and one in that of the Jesuits.

The school of the Jesuits was later turned into a commercial school, under the order of the Salesians. Nikos Kazantzakis, the famous Greek author, studied here and became a great lover of Naxos.

One would expect that these monasteries were founded under the Venetians. Yet not. They were founded during the Ottoman domination. The Venetians were always in a great rivalry with the Pope and did not approve of the strengthening of the Catholic Church in their territories. Therefore, they did not allow the establishment of Catholic monasteries. However, when the Cyclades became finally Ottoman, in 1566, their Catholic population was a good excuse for French kings to intervene in the Ottoman Empire.

Above, the convent of the Ursulines from the side of Aghia Kyriaki church, the favourite of the artists. Below, the monastery of the Capuchins

King Francis had already signed in 1535 a treaty with Sultan Suleiman the Magnificent. According to it, all Catholics of the empire would be under his protection. The French kings sent French monks and nuns, who established monasteries in many islands. Later, when France changed policy, the French were replaced by locals. They keep these institutions until today.

The monastery of the Capuchins

Saint Anthony of Padua, the church of the monastery of the Capuchins

Some of them housed schools, which later became so famous for the good French education they offered, that they attracted pupils from as far as Madagascar. However, initially, they were the first schools in these islands since ancient times. Perhaps King Francis had not the most altruistic motives, but we must admit that he offered a great service to the Cyclades and beyond.

Convent of the Ursulines

The kitchen of the convent of the Ursulines

The Naxos convent of the Ursulines was founded in 1670 by local women of the Castle. Later, they were joined by French nuns. It was the first school for girls founded not only in Greece but also throughout the

Eastern Mediterranean! It operated for exactly 300 years, until 1970.

These schools fell, unfortunately, victims to the massive displacement of the inhabitants to Athens after World War II. The Ursulines, however, continue their educational tradition at the new schools that were established in the capital. Today, the building complex in Naxos houses the cultural centre 'Saint Ursula'.

The cultural centre 'Saint Ursula'

5. Museums in the Castle

Inside the Castle, we also saw the Archaeological Museum, housed in the former Jesuit monastery. Apart from the other very important exhibits, the collection of Cycladic figurines is the second largest after that of the National Archaeological Museum of Athens. Naxos occupied a prominent position in Prehistory, thanks to its size and central location in the Aegean Sea. The islands of the Aegean acted as a bridge uniting Europe to Asia and profited from the commercial activities between these lands, their ports receiving the ships that ensured that trade.

The third millennium BC, i.e. the Early Bronze Age, was the era of the so-called Cycladic civilization, which created these astonishing figurines. These works of art in local white marble impress by their abstract forms, which inspired many modern artists. At that time, Naxos had a dense population, installed in small settlements along the island's coast.

The courtyard of the Archaeological Museum (former Jesuit monastery)

However, the settlements of the Cycladic civilization had a violent end, which resulted in the interruption of this artistic creation. Around 2000 BC, the Cyclades started being influenced by the Minoan civilization of Crete, the new emerging power in the Aegean Sea. That led to a new period of prosperity in the Cyclades, which ended with the decline of Crete around 1500 BC and the arrival of the Mycenaeans, who dominated the last phase of Bronze Age in Greece.

Cycladic figurines in the Archaeological Museum of Naxos. Photo by Zde / CC BY-SA (https://creativecommons.org/licenses/by-sa/3.0)

Another museum we visited was the Venetian Museum, in the Dellarocca-Barozzi mansion. It has very interesting furniture and objects that give a lot of information about the history of Naxos. However, the Dellarocca-Barozzi is not the only Venetian mansion. Walking in the Castle, we saw many others that still preserve their escutcheons. Since the Castle buildings have retained their use (residential and religious buildings), the medieval fortified city seems to have remained untouched by time. Walking through the winding streets, you think the Duke of the Archipelago will appear around some corner.

photo by Denis Roubien

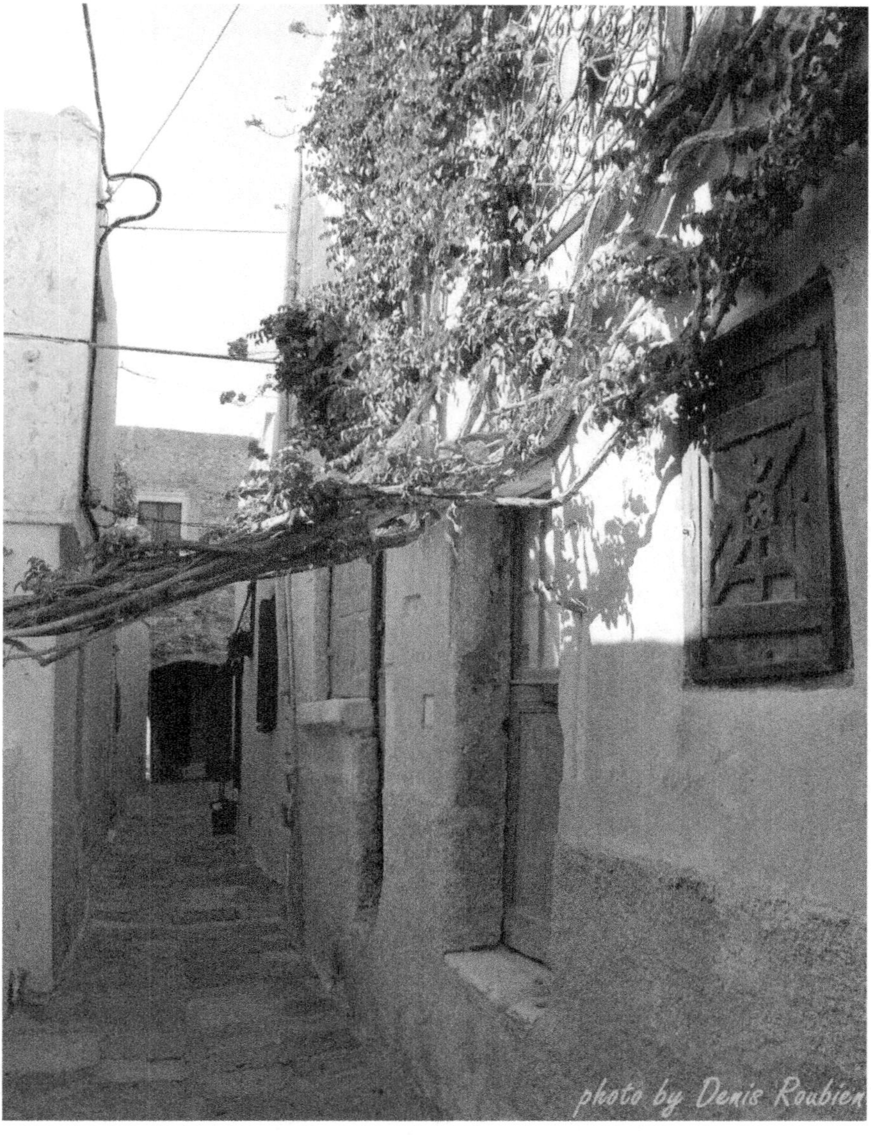
photo by Denis Roubien

6. Around the Castle

Outside the Castle, you can complete your visit with two other monuments of Venetian times. One is the church of Saint Anthony the Hermit, in the harbour. From the outside, it looks like a typical Cycladic church. Nevertheless, inside it's Gothic. It was built around 1440 and later given to the Knights of Rhodes (Knights Hospitaller). That is why we see their characteristic cross at the entrance.

Saint Anthony. A typical Cycladic church from outside, Gothic inside. At the entrance, the cross of the Knights Hospitaller

The other Venetian monument is the small church of the Virgin Mary of the Snow, in the market. Its strange name is linked to a tradition of Rome. On the night of August 4th to August 5th 356, the Virgin Mary appeared in a dream to a Roman nobleman named John and asked him to build a basilica at the place where it would have snowed in the morning.

Pope Liberius had the same dream. After having found out that it had actually snowed on one of the Seven Hills of Rome, the Esquilin, he ordered the construction of a church in honour of the Virgin Mary. They named the church Santa Maria ad Nives, namely, the Virgin Mary of the Snow. Later they built there one of the largest churches in the world and one of the most important monuments of Rome: Santa Maria Maggiore. The church of Naxos, of course, is just a Cycladic chapel. At first sight, however, because if you notice carefully you will see various details that again reveal the island's unique past.

The interior of Saint Anthony

The Virgin Mary of the Snow

7. A unique museum

Before leaving Chora, we visited the Site Museum, opposite the Orthodox cathedral of Zoodochos Pighi (Source of Life, built in 1787). It is a museum unique in Greece and one of very few of its kind in the whole world. Here, the exhibits are the findings which have been kept in the excavation site. They date from two periods: first, from the Mycenaean period (1300-1100 BC). After the decline of the Minoan civilization of Crete, which had greatly influenced the Cyclades, the islands played the role of a bridge for the expansion of the Mycenaean civilization, which had the city of Mycenae in the Peloponnese as its centre and dominated Greece at that time. An important settlement was then created in today's quarter of Grotta, where this museum is situated. From that period, we can see a part of the city's walls and little pottery workshops, including non-baked pots placed on tables, basins once containing paints for the pots and a pottery kiln.

The Geometric period (900-700 BC) followed the two centuries of chaos that was engendered by the arrival of the Dorians in about 1100 BC and the subsequent fall of the Mycenaean civilization. Naxos is now mainly inhabited by Ionians who came from Attica and occupies once again a prominent position among the Greek powers. At that time, the use of this place changed and it became a sanctuary. A tumulus was created, which covered the tombs of prominent Naxians. We can still see an offering table with broken pottery around it.

After visiting Chora, we continued our routes in the inland of Naxos, which is a separate world, of an incredible monumental wealth.

Part II. A monumental hinterland

1. The kouroi

I first got to know the hinterland of Naxos by road touring, with the local friend Nikos Gavalas, a member of our hiking group. A few years later, I had the opportunity to discover it by hiking, always under the guidance of Kostas.

Therefore, after the castle of Naxos, now it is the turn of our hiking tour in one of the most monumental hinterlands of the Aegean. First, we will see the antiquities. From all the Cycladic islands, Naxos is the most suitable place to discover archaic Greece, which has prepared the classical world.

In the Archaic period (7th – 6th century BC), which followed the Geometric period, Naxos kept its already established prominent position and became a major naval power. Its economic progress was accompanied by a spectacular prosperity of the arts, and especially sculpture. The existence of marble in the island facilitated this development. The Naxians offered spectacular sculptures in the sanctuaries of Apollo in Delphi and Delos. The god's colossal statue and the famous lions in the Avenue of the Lions in the latter were offered by them. Delos, one of the most important sanctuaries of Greek Antiquity, became a dependence of Naxos, a fact demonstrating the island's importance. The rise of Athens in the 5th century BC marked the end of Naxos's preponderance, since Athens superseded it as the dominant power in the Cyclades. The political decline brought also the loss of its role in the evolution of Greek art.

The top artefacts of archaic sculpture are the kouroi and korai. In Naxos, there are not one, not two, but three kouroi of colossal dimensions. All three are abandoned unfinished in their quarries. It's unknown why they were not completed. Perhaps they are related to the seizure of the orders of wealthy citizens realised by the tyrant Lygdamis as soon as he took over.

Two of them, dating from the 7th century BC, are in Flerio. One in the olive grove of Evdokia Kondyli, who is an attraction herself with her narratives. In her cafe, in the olive grove, she will proudly narrate to you the discovery of the 'Greek' by her grandfather. She will also show you that even foreign guidebooks report her family as a guardian of the kouros, as its size does not allow its transfer to a museum. A similar case is the second kouros of Flerio. This one lies higher and is accessible only by hiking, which we, of course, did.

Above, the kouros in the olive grove of the Kondylis family. Below, the second kouros of Flerio. They both date from the 7th century BC. At the trail Myli - Flerio - Pano Potamia - Mesi Potamia - Kato Potamia

The most impressive, however, is the 6th-century BC kouros near the village of Apollonas. With a length of more than 10 meters, it is the largest. It is also the most 'advanced'. Some features and the beard can be distinguished. Some say it is Dionysus and others say it is Apollo. Some adventurous members of our group climbed up the steep rocks and took 'aerial' photos of it.

The kouros of Apollonas, more than 10 metres long, dating from the 6th century BC

2. The Parthenon was prepared in Naxos

However, it is not just the kouroi. Naxos also has two sanctuaries - among many - of unique archaeological value. One is the sanctuary of Dionysus in Yria. The worship from the 14th to the 8th century BC was outdoors. Four consecutive buildings followed. The restored ruins we see belong to the last temple, of 580 BC (Archaic era). The temples of Yria are of huge archaeological importance, as they document with unique completeness the birth of the marble insular Greek architecture.

Yria, sanctuary of Dionysus, dating from 580 BC

The other great sanctuary is in Gyroulas, near Sangri. Worship began in the 8th century BC and it was also originally outdoors. At the end of the 6th century BC, though, a monumental all-marble temple was built. The sanctuary, according to various indications, was dedicated to Apollo, Demeter and Kore, with an emphasis on their chthonic qualities.

The restored marble temple represents one of the most important steps in the evolution of Greek architecture. Since it is the oldest building where curves were observed, and also the first with marble tiles, it's no exaggeration to say that the Parthenon was prepared here. It is worth visiting not only the temple but also the exemplary museum. It should be noted that the restoration was awarded by the organisation Europa Nostra.

Gyroulas, the restored sanctuary of Apollo, Demeter and Kore, dating from the end of the 6th century BC

However, there are also other archaeological finds. One of the most important is the aqueduct in Melanes. The area of Melanes has plenty of water. That is why the tyrant Lygdamis built an 11-km aqueduct that supplied the ancient city with water.

Above, the ancient aqueduct in Melanes. At the trail Myli - Flerio - Pano Potamia - Mesi Potamia - Kato Potamia. Below, as soon as we approached, mum neighed and called the child by her side, just to be sure...

3. Middle Ages. Naxos closes itself to its interior

After the Archaic period, Naxos lost its significance. Much later, however, in the first Byzantine centuries, monuments of unique value are again created.

The centuries from the 7th to the 9th are called the Dark Ages of Byzantium. After the glorious era of Justinian in the 6th century, the 7th century will see the appearance of the Arabs. The Arab pirates ravaging the coasts force the population, for the first time in Greek history, to withdraw to the hinterland. This is the first time Greece's population centre of gravity shifts from the coast to the interior. As was only natural, attacks by Arab pirates cause great turmoil and lead to a regression of civilisation.

As if that was not enough, in the next two centuries Byzantium is shaken by Iconomachy, the prohibition of religious images. It is a real civil war, which will lead to huge disasters of cultural heritage and not only. As a result of disasters and social unrest, from these three centuries, we have the least information, but also the least monuments and works of art. Nevertheless, Naxos is a strange and unexplained exception to this rule.

Right from this period, Naxos has a great number of monuments that make it again unique throughout Greece. Here is the largest ensemble of churches of Iconomachy. Along with them, an additional great number of Byzantine churches from other periods, which justly gave to Naxos the title of the 'Mystras of the Aegean'.

The majority of these monuments are located on the plateau of Tragaia. Tragaia constitutes the heart of Naxos and almost the entire population gathered here during the 'Dark Ages', to the security of the inland, as far as possible from the dangerous shores. Here you see only a small part of this wealth that we managed to visit in the limited for Naxos time of the six days we had.

As you will notice, the churches of Naxos have a rough structure and no exterior decoration. They are typical monuments of a self-sufficient rural society. That society managed, in times of great shortage of resources in the small Aegean islands, to create its own monuments by the means it had.

Chalki. Aghios Georgios (Saint George) Diasoritis, 11th century

Kerami. Saint John, 13th century

Metochi, near Monitsia. Holy Apostles, 10th-11th century. The only two-storey church in Naxos. At the trail Kaloxylos - Kerami - Akadimi Chalki

Holy Apostles

Rachi. Panaghia (Virgin Mary) Rachidiotissa, 12th-14th century. At the trail Chalki - Panaghia Drosiani

Monitsia. Saint Isidore, 6th-7th century. At the trail Chalki - Panaghia Drosiani. The first school of the Capuchins outside Chora was founded in Monitsia

Monastery of Kaloritsa, near Sangri, 11th-13th century, built over a cave converted into a church in the 4th century. Accessible via a trail from Bazaios tower

4. Panaghia (Virgin Mary) Drosiani
The crown of Naxian churches

The most important of the churches of Naxos is definitely Panaghia Drosiani, in the village of Moni. It dates back to the 6th century, while its frescoes date from the same century and the next. These make it an extremely rare monument. Besides, it has a very special architecture, which arose from additions of different times. You can reach it by hiking from Chalki and passing through many important Byzantine monuments of Tragaia.

With a rough structure and no exterior decoration, Panaghia Drosiani is a typical example of a Naxian church. Its strange shape is the result of additions dating from different times

5. Fotodotis (Giver of Light)
A monastery built like a castle

The oldest monastery in Naxos is the impressive castle - monastery of Christ Fotodotis, which is considered to date from the 6th century. There are many legends and traditions about the monastery's foundation. Most prevalent is the one according to which the monastery was built by a princess. She was endangered by a storm and made a vow to build a church in the land where she would be saved. According to the same tradition, the princess saw some light at this point and, in keeping with her vow, built the monastery dedicated to the 'Giver of Light'.

The tripartite sanctuary betrays that it is not a simple castle. The monastery can be accessed via a trail from Aghia Marina

6. The most important iconoclastic church in Greece

As for the interior, however, the most impressive church in Naxos is Aghia Kyriaki. We approached it by hiking from Apiranthos. In complete contrast to its simple and humble outside, its interior decoration is something unique.

Aghia Kyriaki of Apiranthos. At the trail Apiranthos - Aghia Kyriaki - emery mines - Moutsouna

This is the most important iconoclastic decoration in Greece. An immense variety of shapes and colours compensates for the prohibition to represent sacred persons. Among them are the birds wearing scarves around their necks (!), for which there is no unanimous interpretation. Unfortunately, the publication of photos of this decoration is not allowed by the competent Ephorate of Antiquities.

Aghia Kyriaki of Apiranthos. The humble exterior hides masterpieces

7. In the traces of the crusaders. Naxos after 1204

In 1207, when Naxos is conquered by the crusaders after the fall of the Byzantine Empire, in 1204, the island is divided among several Venetian aristocrats who establish the feudal system of Western Europe. Every nobleman exploits a part of the island. In this, he builds his tower where he resides in order to control the exploitation of his lands.

Even after the formal incorporation of Naxos into the Ottoman Empire, in 1566, with the death of the last Duke, the feudal system survived until 1830, with the foundation of the Greek State. The difference after 1566 was that in some cases Greek rulers replaced the Venetians and took the Venetian towers or built their own.

Despite the toughness of the Venetian administration, the naval power of Venice reduced insecurity due to piracy. Therefore, the population and the settlements grew. That is why, as in the other Cyclades, the old settlements present today mainly the form they took during the Venetian occupation.

The Fragopoulos - Dellarocca tower in Kourounochori. In the background, Melanes. In the centre of the tower's façade is the murder hole. From here, they poured boiling water on the invaders

8. Apiranthos. A Cretan touch in the heart of the Cyclades

Our routes could not leave Apiranthos out of the way. A special village, both for its beauty and for its cultural specificity. The local dialect suggests that the village was inhabited by Cretans, who must have arrived here as refugees. Moreover, as if that was not enough, there are five museums to see here!

Apiranthos. Zevgolis tower (17th century) and Saint Anthony

Apiranthos. Saint Anthony

Apiranthos. The main street

Hiking from Apiranthos to the emery mines and Moutsouna. Because Naxos also has mineral wealth. Emery was loaded at the port of Moutsouna

Kokkos tower, 17th century. At the trail Myli - Flerio - Pano Potamia - Mesi
Potamia - Kato Potamia

Kokkos tower

9. Kaloxylos - Kerami - Akadimi – Chalki
Hiking through the villages of Tragaia

This hiking route is ideal for exploring the villages of Tragaia.

Kaloxylos

Kaloxylos

Kaloxylos

Kaloxylos

Akadimi. Markopolitis tower, 18th century

Akadimi. Markopolitis tower, 18th century

Seeing Filoti, the largest village of the Cyclades, while hiking

10. Chalki. The noble capital of Tragaia

Our hiking route in the Tragaia plateau brings us to Chalki. Capital of the island before the arrival of the Venetians, Chalki has always been the centre of the rich plateau of Tragaia.

In Chalki, we participated in a guided tour of the Vallindras distillery, which since 1896 makes the famous citrus liqueur. As they explained to us, the citrus is made from leaves and not from fruit, as one would expect, judging from other liqueurs.

The position of Chalki as the 'capital' of Tragaia is demonstrated by the functions it houses. In the central square, there is even a gallery. More precisely, the photographer's Dimitris Gavalas gallery. From what he said to us, the animation of Chalki supports the presence of the gallery here, instead of Chora, for example, as anyone who does not know would think.

Approaching Chalki on foot. Tower of Barozzi - Grazia - Fragopoulos (17th century)

Chalki. The next image we see: Virgin Mary the Protothronos. Iconoclastic church of the 9th century. Inside, it has a synthronon (embedded stalls), rare feature in churches after the Early Christian period (4th-6th century)

Chalki. We are now entering the village. Chalki is characterised by its neoclassical architecture, which gives it a special nobility

Chalki. Above, the square. Below, the scarcity of space in the fortified medieval settlements made such interventions in the buildings' angles necessary, in order to permit the passage of loaded mules. The rather Arab decorative motive could be an import of Naxian seamen

11. Leaving Tragaia

Bazaios tower. It was built in 1600 as a monastery of the Holy Cross and functioned until the early 19th century. Now it houses cultural activities

Aghia tower, 17th century

Aghia monastery, dedicated to the Virgin Mary. Accessible via a trail from Aghia tower

Koronos. Here we discovered another Naxos, mountainous and inaccessible, with its own beauty

Filoti. Barozzi tower, 17th century

Filoti. The coat of arms of the Barozzi, at the entrance of the tower of the same name

12. Jesuit resort. The abandoned monument

Hiking from the village of Melanes, we reached the Jesuit resort at Kalamitsia. It is a huge complex, built in the 17th century. It served as the resting place of the Jesuit missionaries who were running through the countryside of Naxos. Today, unfortunately, it remains unused and abandoned to its fate.

13. Portara. Transition to another dimension

And now a reversal in the chronological order of the monuments.

Since we left in the afternoon, when the sun began to set, the ideal setting to say goodbye to Naxos was Portara. Portara is on the small island of Palatia, united with Naxos. According to mythology, Theseus left Ariadne here on the way from Crete to Athens. Here Dionysus found her and married her. Here, they said, the first Dionysian Mysteries (feast in honour of Dionysus) took place.

Portara is a remnant of the incomplete colossal temple of Apollo. The tyrant Lygdamis attempted to build it in the 6th century BC, the age of the peak of ancient Naxos. Here you can see the island's most famous sunset. Here we 'walked through' the door leading out of Naxos. Not for long though. We renewed the appointment to try to discover more things from the countless ones that this island of unique cultural richness has to offer.

Chora seen form the island of Palatia, where we went to see one of the most famous sunsets in Greece

Portara, a remnant of the incomplete colossal temple of Apollo (6th century BC) on the islet of Palatia

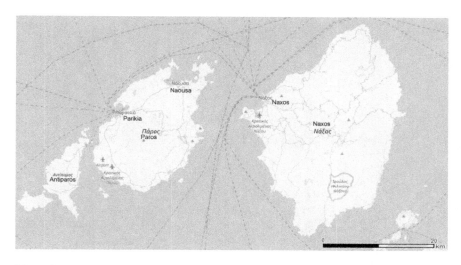

Map of Naxos, with Paros and Antiparos

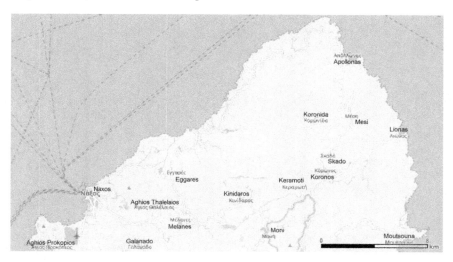

Map of northern Naxos

Map of central Naxos

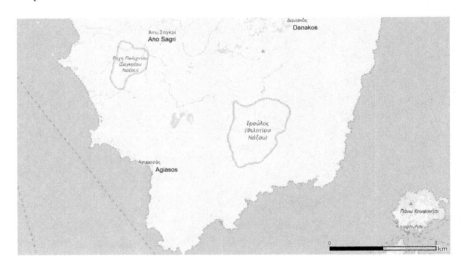

Map of southern Naxos

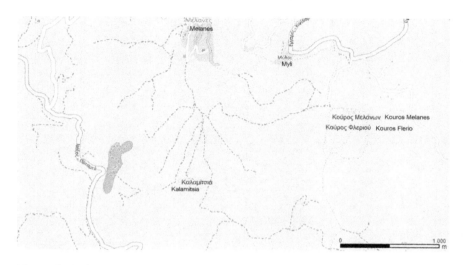

The trails Myli - Flerio and Melanes - Kalamitsia

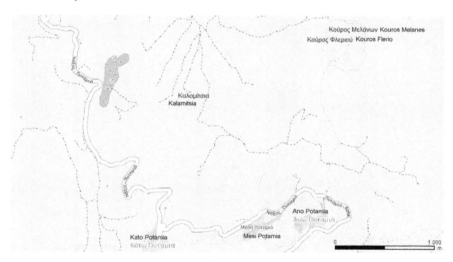

The trail Flerio - Ano Potamia - Mesi Potamia - Kato Potamia

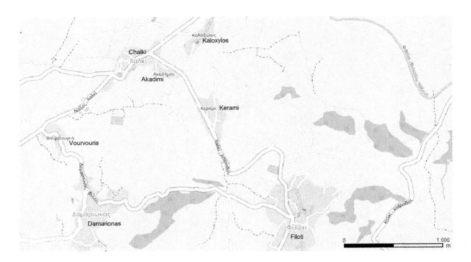

The trail Kaloxylos - Kerami - Akadimi - Chalki

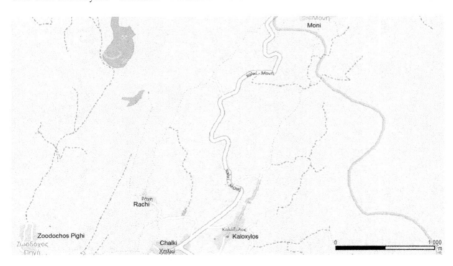

The trail Chalki - Moni (Panaghia Drosiani)

76

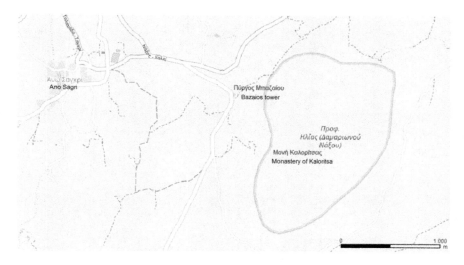

The trail Bazaios tower - monastery of Kaloritsa

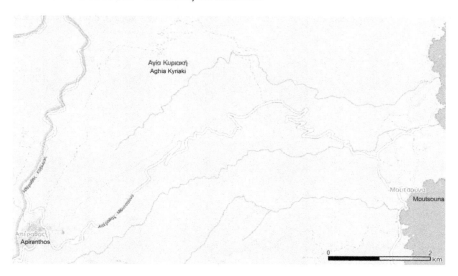

The trail Apiranthos - Aghia Kyriaki – Moutsouna

Tinos
The last jewel
in the crown of Venice

Part I. The last bastion of the western world in the Aegean

1. Tinos. For how many days?

'You are staying five days in Tinos?!' Said the middle-aged lady in the hotel restaurant to Fani, a member of our hiking group. 'What are you going to do here five entire days? You will visit the Virgin Mary, you will eat a galaktoboureko in Pyrgos, and then what?'

She could not imagine that, for us, five days would not be enough to discover the most misunderstood island of the Cyclades. Yet, until recently, it was the most visited one. Until the recent explosion of tourism, it had more visitors annually than Mykonos and Santorini, its world-famous neighbours. It seems incredible, but it has a simple explanation.

Almost all visitors who flock to Tinos do as our astonished hotel acquaintance: they go for a pilgrimage to the most celebrated religious destination of Greece: Megalochari, the Virgin Mary of the Great Grace. They usually descend from the ship and go immediately to the church. After the necessary time in it, a short stop at one of the main avenue's shops to buy a souvenir, usually the icon of their favourite saint. And then back to the boat and to Piraeus, after a 5-hour trip. Often without spending the night on the island, in order to minimize the cost.

Above, Megalochari, the Virgin Mary of the Great Grace, on its celebration day, 25th of March. The greatest pilgrimage in Greece. Below, the 'unknown' Megalochari: the sanctuary

2. A little beyond Megalochari

The most adventurous ones go as far as making the classic short tourist trip. First, a visit to the convent of Kechrovouni, to pay homage to the nun-saint Pelagia.

The best-preserved medieval settlement, with no subsequent additions. In fact, it is the convent of Kechrovouni

In 1823, during the Greek Revolution, Pelagia said she had a vision. The Virgin Mary revealed to her that an icon of hers was on a hill next to the port. Sure enough, the icon was found there and a sumptuous shrine emerged at the same place immediately afterwards. The Greeks considered this a favourable omen for the outcome of the Revolution. Thus, the icon became the most venerated religious object in Greece.

After the convent, perhaps a visit to Pyrgos, the only village known to more than a few people. Apart from its beauty, it owes its fame to its great marble sculptors. They have created some of the best works of art of modern Greece. There, in the little village square, under the shade of trees, they will taste the famous galaktoboureko mentioned by our acquaintance, a sweet filled with cream.

The convent of Kechrovouni is like a particularly well-tended village

But even those who venture to Pyrgos, at the other end of the island, soon return to their boat. To go back home and be able thereafter to say that they, too, have visited the sacred island.

Kostas, the chief of our group, smiled indulgently when he heard the comment that could have been said by almost anyone of the island's visitors. "Tinos has about forty old villages, but we will traverse 'only' 24 of them. All of them are beautiful, but, unfortunately, they are not all suitable for hiking", he said. Since he has been hiking in Greece for decades, always adding new destinations to the souvenir album of his adepts, we had to take his word for it.

This is another surprise. Forty old villages? If you open any book on the Aegean islands and especially the Cyclades, you will always read the same thing: that, for centuries, the few inhabitants that survived the continuous pirate attacks had to nestle on the most inaccessible rock, to save their lives. In most islands, they were no more than a few hundred, so they had to stick together in one village. In the largest islands, they afforded to build little more than one. But forty? That sounds incredible.

3. Historical explanations

You already suspect something is different on this island. If you want to understand it, Father Markos is your best option. Whether you prefer to read his books before coming, in order to surprise your unsuspecting travel mates, or you prefer personal contact.

I preferred the latter and learned a lot of interesting things. He is probably the island's most prolific historian and is responsible for the archives of the Catholic Archdiocese of Naxos and Tinos. Yes, that is right. A Catholic Archdiocese on the island housing the greatest Greek Orthodox pilgrimage, in a country of an overwhelming Orthodox majority. Again, there is a perfectly good explanation.

In 1207, three years after the crusaders of the fourth crusade conquered the Byzantine Empire, Marco Sanudo, a Venetian nobleman, and nephew of the doge Enrico Dandolo, seized most of the Cyclades. He created the Duchy of the Archipelago and settled in Naxos.

Tinos and Mykonos, though, were not part of this state. That same year they came under the two Venetian brothers Andrea and Geremia Ghisi and their heirs. That lasted until 1390 when Venice undertook their direct administration. The rest of the Cyclades were conquered by the Ottomans in 1537 and officially annexed by the Ottoman Empire in 1566, with the death of the last Duke of the Archipelago. However, Venice managed to keep Tinos until as late as 1715. That was partly thanks to Xobourgo, the highest fortress of the Aegean, 641 metres high.

Needless to say, from up there we had a magnificent view. Not only the whole island could be seen, but also many others around it. Thanks to Xobourgo, Tinos became Venice's last possession in the Aegean. And, by extension, the last bastion of the Western world in the Eastern Mediterranean.

The highest fortress of the Aegean. Thanks to it, Venice kept Tinos for more than five centuries. Xobourgo with the village of Tripotamos at its feet

Looking down from Xobourgo. Xinara

Looking down from Xobourgo. Koumaros and, in the background, Volax

Looking far away from Xobourgo. Ktikados. As Ktikados is a mixed village, two churches dominate its horizon: on the left the Orthodox one of Panaghia Megalomata, and on the right the Catholic one of the Holy Cross

Looking far away from Xobourgo. Kampos and, behind it, Tarabados

Looking far away from Xobourgo. Falatados

Looking far away from Xobourgo. From left to right: Steni, Mesi, Kechros, Tzados

Looking far away from Xobourgo. Tripotamos and, in the background, Chora

4. An island with a special cultural identity

When Greece was conquered by the crusaders, most of the inhabitants remained Orthodox. Catholicism was mostly represented by the feudal aristocracy of the conquerors. However, Tinos and Syros were an exception to that rule. Here, the majority of the population followed the conquerors' religion. And although this is well-known for Syros, very fewer people know the case of Tinos.

This is because the bulk of Syros's mixed population lives in its port. And since this is also the capital of the Cyclades, it makes the particularity of Syros too obvious to be missed. On the contrary, this part of Tinos's identity is to be found in a constellation of villages, well hidden from the uninitiated eye in the island's interior. The second reason is that the pilgrimage to Megalochari almost eclipsed anything else.

Since my aim is to present less known aspects of known destinations, we will first focus on the Inner Parts of Tinos (Mesa Meri). This is the island's central and eastern portion, containing most of the medieval villages. Their name is in opposition to the island's farthest side, the Outer Parts (Exo Meri). The Inner Parts are additionally divided into the Upper and the Lower Parts (Pano Meri and Kato Meri).

'How many of you live here?' One of our group asked the old man who came out of his house to greet us in the little village of Loutra (Baths). 'Ten at this moment. Many more will come from Easter onward'.

It is late March and we suspect that what we see is the ordinary image of this village most of the year. We got similar answers in every other village, apart from some large ones, like Komi, Triantaros, or Falatados. Most of the island's inhabitants have moved mainly to Athens. They come here only in summer if they still work, or from Easter to early fall if they have retired.

And yet, Tinos had once as many as 28,000 inhabitants, when Naxos, the archipelago's largest island, had no more than 6,000, according to old-times travellers. Who could imagine that Loutra, this village of ten permanent inhabitants had once a world-famous girls' school of as many as 300 pupils?

5. A school of international range

The explanation for these overwhelming numbers is again to be found in the island's history. After the Cyclades became Ottoman, at last, their Catholic population was a good pretext for King Francis I of France to interfere in the Ottoman Empire. He had already signed a treaty with Sultan Suleiman the Magnificent. According to it, all the Catholics of the Empire would be under his protection. That partly explains why Tinos acquired such a population. Because it became a shelter for the persecuted from all over Greece.

The French kings sent French monks and nuns, who founded monasteries and convents on many islands. When France later changed its politics, the French were replaced by locals. They keep these institutions until today. Some of them housed schools. These became later so famous for offering good French education, that they attracted pupils from as far as Madagascar. However, at their beginning, they were the first schools on these islands since ancient times. Perhaps King Francis did not have the most selfless motives. Nevertheless, we have to admit that he offered a great service to the Cyclades and not only them.

In Tinos, that school was precisely in Loutra and administered by the Ursulines. The convent exists still, but the school fell, alas, victim to the massive move of the inhabitants to Athens after World War II. The nuns continue their educational tradition in the new schools they founded in the capital and the school in Loutra became a museum. There, guided by a local girl, we discovered the incredibly high level of education it once offered to its pupils.

But the small village of Loutra has yet more to offer. It was not only the Ursulines who observed its beauty, but also the Jesuits. Their large monastery of Saint Joseph has a museum of folk art. In it, we discovered an astonishing collection of tools, agricultural equipment, and much more. Among its exhibits, no one overlooked the 'machine' of making 'petroto', the island's exquisite cheese. During the production procedure, it is pressed with a heavy stone (petra in Greek), which explains its name.

Loutra. The convent of the Ursulines, with its world-famous girls' school

Loutra. Convent of the Ursulines. The painting classroom

91

Above, a monumental urban ensemble amid the fields. Jesuit monastery of Saint Joseph in Loutra. In the background, Krokos Below, the folk art museum in the Jesuit monastery

6. Perfectly preserved medieval settlements

Apart from their religious buildings, the medieval villages of Tinos are typical Cycladic settlements. But usually of the most beautiful kind.

In the village of Dyo Choria (which actually means Two Villages) I remembered what I had read in a history book. An eighteenth-century British traveller had reported that when he arrived here, he had to have his mule unloaded. Otherwise, it could not pass through the village's main street. He asked the locals what was the fastest way for him to traverse the village. They advised him to go from one roof to the other. And in fact, this is where most of them were at the moment, participating in a celebration since the village had literally no open space.

For protection against pirates, the locals built their houses attached to one another. Thus, they formed a continuous outer front, with no openings, like a fortification. The lack of space was such, that they even built parts of their houses above the streets.

The ideal place to see how the Cycladic settlements were at the time of piracy when they were not whitewashed so that they could not be seen is Monastiria because it is an abandoned village. The only 'dissonance' is the church of Saint Joseph

Monastiria

Monastiria

An elegant solution to the scarcity of space in medieval villages. Loutra

Another elegant solution to the scarcity of space in medieval villages. Xinara

Above, a kapasos (chimney made of an upside-down pot) in Komi. Below, one of the countless auxiliary buildings decorating the countryside of Tinos. Near Perastra, on the trail Loutra - Perastra - Komi

The huge slabs of Tinos allow even the construction of ceilings. Tarabados

Kampos, as seen from the trail from Tarabados. One of the settlements that preserved their compact character

7. Discovering the hospitality of Tinos

Triantaros, below, and Dyo Choria, above. Subsequent additions give the impression that the dense medieval cores no longer exist

All the island's medieval villages are still like this, but they are usually surrounded by more recent and more aerated parts. That gives a false impression that what the British traveller describes no longer exists. That was our first impression when we arrived at the main square of Dyo Choria, immediately out of the dense medieval core.

It was then that a hospitable lady materialized from nowhere, bringing a jug of homemade lemonade along with cups, enough for the whole group, about fifteen people. She was the only living soul we saw in this large village, but appearances were deceptive. Wherever we went, there were always people coming out of their houses to greet us. They all seemed very happily surprised to see visitors when they least expected them. Some of them offered us treats, like dates in Tripotamos and chocolates in Kardiani.

Above, Arnados, next to Dyo Choria. Below, the central square in Dyo Choria. The dense medieval settlement is hidden behind it

8. The most beautiful houses for... non-humans

Beautiful houses are not to be found only in villages, but also out of them. Out of the village of Tarabados, we came across perhaps the most enviable ensemble of massive housing for... non-humans.

I am of course talking of the famous dovecotes of Tinos, which are said to be more than one thousand. They are to be found all over the Inner Parts, but Tarabados offers the greatest concentration of them. Moreover, there is a long trail going along them. Following that trail, we exclaimed more than once how lucky these pigeons are, to live in such houses. Until they are eaten, of course, we thought afterwards. Anyway, when I showed photos of them to foreign colleagues of mine, they could not believe these constructions are made for pigeons. They told me they seemed to them too luxurious even for humans.

The most enviable ensemble of massive housing for... non-humans. On the trail of the dovecotes in Tarabados

Tarabados again

Humans and pigeons lodging together. Berdemiaros

Mountados. On the trail Mountados - Sbirados - Tripotamos

Maybe Tarabados offers the most spectacular ensemble of dovecotes. However, the prize for the most beautifully situated must go to an isolated one, midway on the trail to Agapi (the Greek word for 'love'). The small waterfall at its feet makes it really unique. Yes, a waterfall. The arid Cyclades, when visited in winter or spring, after a period of rain, can have even waterfalls.

A waterfall in the Cyclades. Near Agapi, on the trail Volax - Agapi

9. Modernism in the Middle Ages

Afterwards, the trail led us to a valley of many more dovecotes and the village of Agapi at its end. And behind our backs, dominating the valley, we saw the most modernist medieval church you can imagine.

Agapi, the valley with the dovecotes, as we arrive from Volax

It is the chapel of Saint Sophia, supposed to date from the 10th century. Apart from its very interesting interior mural paintings, the exterior looks as if it were the very inspiration of Le Corbusier, the famous modernist Swiss architect.

In his writings, he claims that the whitewashed chapels he saw in the Cyclades inspired him greatly in his work, especially the chapel of Notre Dame du Haut in Ronchamp, France. However, I very much doubt he ever saw this particular chapel. Hiking in the hidden valleys of Tinos was very unlikely to come to his mind as a means of discovering the island.

More the pity, since he would no doubt have been thrilled by the harmonic asymmetry of its façade. In my opinion, this is a masterpiece of abstract art and, I have to admit, my favourite church in Tinos. Maybe this does not do justice to the monumental Baroque churches of the Inner Parts or to the marble masterpieces of the Outer Parts that you can see even in the smallest village, but there it is.

Above, Saint Sophia in Agapi, on the trail from Volax. Le Corbusier would have loved this 10th-century modernist church. Below, the view from Saint Sophia: Sklavochorio, the only Orthodox village in the Lower Parts

10. The magnificence of the Italian baroque in little Tinos

Agapi, the church of Saint Agapitos. There could be no greater contrast to Saint Sophia, which we saw shortly before reaching the village

And this is another curious thing. Among the island's thousand churches (as many as the dovecotes), most rural chapels are the well-known whitewashed cubes so enthusiastically described by Le Corbusier.

But the large parish churches in the villages seem to come from another part of the planet. To be exact, they come from Italy. Italy gave religious architectural models not only to the Catholics of Tinos but often also to their Orthodox neighbours, especially in mixed villages.

At first sight, the most impressive example is the cathedral of the Virgin Mary of the Rosary. This is in the particularly beautiful village of Xinara (which means big fountain in the local vocabulary).

A small village with an unexpectedly majestic church. Saint John in Skalados. Probably the oldest tall bell tower of Tinos (1792). Opposite, the village of Smardakito

A large Baroque cathedral amid the fields. The Virgin Mary of the Rosary in Xinara

The façade of the cathedral of the Virgin Mary of the Rosary in Xinara

Saint Zachary in Kalloni. Many say it is the largest church in Tinos (photo by Markisia Armaou)

Another majestic Baroque church in the fields. Assumption of the Virgin Mary in Kato Klisma

Holy Cross in Ktikados

Not only Baroque but also leaning. Karkados, Transfiguration. Also known as little Pisa

A bit of Baroque Rome in the heart of the Cyclades. Saint Anne in Perastra. On the trail Loutra - Perastra - Komi. Below, a house in Komi. A very rare appearance of Baroque in secular architecture

Krokos with the Baroque church of Evangelistria (Virgin Mary of the Annunciation) and above it the equally Baroque chapel of the Assumption of the Virgin Mary in Plakakia, outside Skalados

Saint Michael in Tarabados

Saint George in Perastra. A much simpler version

A rare and very interesting coupling of 'formal' and traditional architecture. Pilgrimage of the Sacred Heart in Xobourgo (initially, the monastery of the Jesuits until their installation in Loutra). The elegant traditional little dome at the side aisle constitutes a 'melodic dissonance' in the strict formal architecture of the whole

The Presentation of the Virgin Mary in Tripotamos. In Tinos, even Orthodox churches are often Baroque

Panaghia Megalomata (large-eyed-Virgin-Mary) in Ktikados. Another Orthodox church with Baroque influences

However, I think that the most important example of this influence is not that obvious.

11. An unknown masterpiece

Franciscan monastery of Saint Anthony of Padua. The usual for Tinos Baroque façade hides a surprise

If you are really intrigued, do not lose the opportunity to visit the Franciscan church of Saint Anthony of Padua in Chora, the port. Do not stop at its façade and say 'Oh my God, I can't take any more Baroque! I came here to see a simple Cycladic island with just a whitewashed village and beaches and I keep seeing monuments everywhere!'

Instead, go inside and turn to the left. There, you will see a miniature of Michelangelo's Laurentian Library in Florence. Observe the quality of the work and think of the date of its completion: 1747, when most of Greece was occupied by the Ottomans and almost completely cut out from the rest of Europe. That will persuade you that this island must have been a cultural hub.

And if the church is closed, do not hesitate to ask the Catholic Archdiocese, next to it, to send someone to open it for you. This is what we did and a very kind lady from Kalloni opened the church for us. Do not forget, the hospitality of this island's inhabitants is beyond description.

The little sister of Michelangelo's Laurentian Library. Saint Anthony of Padua in Chora

12. The hidden beauty of Chora

Chora, as seen from Poles. On the trail Ktikados - Chora

To reward you for the trouble you took to discover this place, one of my personal favourites, I will give you a tip. Behind this Franciscan monastery extends Pallada, Chora's most beautiful quarter. I assure you it will change your mind if you thought this insular capital city is less attractive than others. There, among some very beautiful neoclassical houses, you will find some very good restaurants offering the island's delicious local food. Do not miss the famous artichokes and louza, the local salted pork. The local cheese goes without saying.

Who said the capital city of Tinos is not that attractive? Wrong!

Chora, Saint Nicholas

Chora, Saint Nicholas

13. From Mexico to Tinos

Back to the island's interior, I advise you to let your steps lead you to Pentostrato, next to the villages of Mesi and Steni. There, you will find another unique church. I know you cannot take more Baroque than a normal human being can in such a short time. Nevertheless, this one is different. I will hint that it is a kind of church unique not only in Greece but also perhaps in the whole of Europe.

A Mexican church lost in the Cyclades. Saint Francis in Pentostrato

Does it intrigue you to see a Mexican church in the middle of a Cycladic island? Then do not miss the 18th-century Franciscan monastery of Saint Francis. It looks nothing like anything else around it. For mysterious reasons, it looks very much like the Franciscan (again) mission churches in New Mexico. Until now, no one has given an explanation for this transplant. If we consider that the Mexican churches are made of mud bricks, which explains the form and thickness of their walls and buttresses, the exact transplant of these forms into stone architecture, as is the case here, becomes even more inexplicable.

The rear part of Saint Francis's church

The view from Saint Francis. The combined churches of Taxiarches (the Archangels) and Saint. Michael, near the village of Mesi

Not far from Saint Francis, another mysterious spectacle: hiking from Falatados to Volax through Kathlikaros, we stumbled upon the church of the Assumption of the Virgin Mary, at the cemetery of Falatados. Below the bell tower, we distinguished two mysterious figures, reminiscent of the pre-Columbian civilizations of America!

The Assumption of the Virgin Mary, at the cemetery of Falatados

The bell tower of the Assumption of the Virgin Mary, at the cemetery of Falatados, with mysterious figures reminiscent of the pre-Columbian civilizations of America

14. Natural particularities as well

Leaving Falatados and hiking towards Volax. Falatados is dominated by the church of Saint John the Theologian and the Holy Trinity, with the marble façade

And if you have had too much culture, I have something different for you now, again unique, at least in Greece. I know, you are exasperated by so many unique things on this island. This last thing I will mention in the Inner Parts is a natural wonder. If you follow the trail from Falatados to Volax, you will arrive at an area full of thousands of round rocks.

The mysterious rocks on the trail from Falatados to Volax

Opinions differ as to their origin. Some experts say they were at the bottom of the sea when this area was immersed in Prehistoric times. Others say they are meteorites. Whichever is true, it is a sight you will not forget. Especially if you arrive at Volax (which actually means large pebble) and discover that its houses are built on some of these rocks, which stick out of their walls.

Volax. The houses are built on the mysterious rocks

photo by Denis Roubien

We finish our tour in the Inner Parts mentioning that, apart from all this cultural wealth, there are also beautiful beaches as in all Greek islands.

Do not think Tinos does not have wonderful beaches, like any island. This is Kolybithra

Part II. A tour of Phidias's part of the world

1. Kardiani. First taste of the Outer Parts

And now to the Outer Parts…

We enter Kardiani at dusk. Kardiani is the first village one meets on the way from the Inner to the Outer Parts. Therefore, it seems to be the link between the two areas of Tinos. Here it is still green as in the Inner Parts. And very green at that. We have not yet arrived at the marble areas, where vegetation is typically scarce.

Also the Baroque we saw in abundance in the Inner Parts still exists. And exactly here it makes its last appearance. And not just in the Catholic churches of Our Lady Kioura and the Assumption of the Virgin Mary, but also in the Orthodox church of the Holy Trinity. Because Kardiani constitutes a link from this point of view too. It is a mixed village, the only one in the Outer Parts with a Catholic population. Therefore, this is the last place of a strong Venetian imprint.

Kardiani overlooks the sea, with its three major churches. In the front, Our Lady Kioura

And since it is the last place, the imprint is intense. Therefore, the Baroque reigns in all three major churches. Perhaps it is the only village of Tinos with three large churches. All three face the sea. Because Kardiani is one of the few villages that dared, in the age of piracy, be erected on the mountain brow and seen from the sea. Thanks to the courage of their ancestors, modern inhabitants have the rare privilege of contemplating the sea from their homes.

Kardiani, Holy Trinity. While Orthodox, this one too is Baroque, like the other two

Holy Trinity. Marble façade and marble steeple. The curtain in the sanctuary is also made of marble!

However, there is something that betrays that we got to the Outer Parts: marble. The marble façade and marble steeple of the Holy Trinity and the marble parts of Kioura worthily represent the local marble-sculpting tradition. Here begins Tinos of the artists.

Above, a characteristic imaginative Cycladic jardinière in Kardiani. Below, Kardiani, Assumption of the Virgin Mary

Kardiani, a sculpture of stone and lime

It is Mrs. Theresia who opens Our Lady Kioura for us. During the Venetian domination, Kioura-Kardiani (= Our Lady of hearts) was a pilgrimage of the whole Tinos. It gathered a large number of pilgrims, Catholic and Orthodox. Two shrines coexisted, one for each community.

Eventually, the church came to the Catholic community of the village of Kardiani, which had been built in the early 17th century. Therefore, but also due to the great distance that separated the area from all the other Catholic villages in the Inner Parts, the pilgrimage lost its general character.

The next day, when we go back, Mrs. Theresia, faithful to the spirit of treats we also met in other villages, 'forces' us to empty a bag of chocolates. And when we leave, she asks with which ship we leave Tinos. And she promises to greet us with signals she will make to us with her 'little mirror'.

The bell tower of Our Lady Kioura. The Baroque apotheosis in Kardiani

Kardiani, Our Lady Kioura

2. Arriving at the first artistic centre. Ysternia

We say goodbye to Kardiani and reach Ysternia. Ysternia is another 'courageous' village overlooking the sea. And it is exactly from there that we come. We climbed from the Bight of Ysternia (Ormos Ysternion) through a paved trail made by unknown artists. Here we are in the Outer Parts for good. The Baroque ends, the vegetation diminishes, and marble multiplies. Nevertheless, here the style is different.

Ysternia, Saint Paraskevi, with its imposing marble façade. The building that stands out in the village

As we said previously, in the Outer Parts, all villages except Kardiani are Orthodox. This region is the farthest from the administrative and economic centres of the island during the Venetian domination. Therefore, the Venetian imprint fades. Thus, the architecture is more familiar, reminding of other parts of Greece.

photo by Denis Roubien

Except, of course, for the materials. Because the materials reveal another imprint: the imprint of Phidias. According to an ancient tradition, which is not absolutely certain, Phidias came from Tinos. It is possible that the tradition was created because of the marble quarries, which have been known since antiquity. Regardless of that, the many contemporary Phidias coming from the Outer Parts of Tinos justify the ancient tradition.

photo by Denis Roubien

3. In the capital of the artists. Pyrgos, marble everywhere

Arriving at Pyrgos through a trail from Venardados

After Ysternia, we reach Pyrgos, hiking from Venardados. Across the area, we see a number of 'katikies'. They are small constructions of dry stone, namely, without mortar. The farmers used them in times when travel was difficult. When they had a lot of work, they had no time to return to their village every night. Therefore, they were staying here.

Pyrgos can claim the title of capital of the artists, being the birthplace of most of them. But it is also the birthplace of the one whom many regard as the leading artist of modern Greece: Yannoulis Chalepas (1851-1938).

Rightly, then, in Pyrgos is located the School of Marble Crafts, which worthily continues the tradition. From here come most of the marble artisans working in the restoration of ancient monuments. Their works above all in the Acropolis will convince you that they are absolutely worthy of their ancient colleagues.

Very naturally, then, Pyrgos is the marble village par excellence. There must be no other village in Greece with so much marble. The most impressive things we saw were the marble fountain in the main square, the churches of Saint Demetrius and Saint Nicholas, and the funerary monuments in the cemetery.

Tomb of Sophia Afentaki, by Yannoulis Chalepas. Athens, First Cemetery. Photo by By LBM1948 - Own work, CC BY-SA 4.0, https://commons.wikimedia.org/w/index.php?curid=79889216

'Katikies' outside Pyrgos

The landscape around Pyrgos

The central square of Pyrgos

The fountain in the central square of Pyrgos. Worthy of the village's tradition

Pyrgos, Saint Nicholas

Pyrgos, Saint Demetrius

Pyrgos, Holy Trinity

154

Unlike the Venetian semi-circular skylights in the Inner Parts, here skylights are square and more recent

And of course, there are museums: the Museum of Tinian artists and the museum housed in the home of Chalepas.

Pyrgos, Museum of Tinian artists

The home-museum of Yannoulis Chalepas

However, the most unexpected is the intercity bus stop. This also is entirely made of marble. This must be international originality.

Pyrgos. Probably the most beautiful bus stop in the world

However, do not take the bus from the marble stop and leave Pyrgos yet. First, you must absolutely visit the amazing Museum of Marble Crafts outside the village. Not only it has very interesting exhibits and an exemplary guided tour and audio-visual presentation of the techniques. But also the building itself is a model of integration in a sensitive natural environment.

4. See you soon

Having visited the Outer Parts as well, we say goodbye to Tinos and sail towards Andros, with the port of Rafina as our final destination. And when the ship is off Kardiani, we look lest we distinguish the signals Mrs. Theresia would make to us with her 'little mirror'.

And we see them. Only we wonder whether it is a little mirror or a full-length one. Did Mrs. Theresia pull out her closet to signal to us with the door mirror? Because the signals are such, that we are certain they are visible from space. Even the aliens may discover Tinos. Who knows... Perhaps this way Tinos will add to its enthusiast fans some more, somewhat more distant...

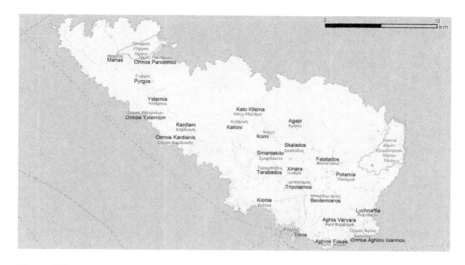

Map of Tinos

The trail Loutra - Perastra - Komi

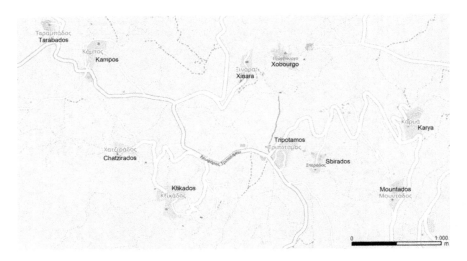

The trail Tarabados - Kampos - Ktikados

The trail Mountados - Sbirados - Tripotamos

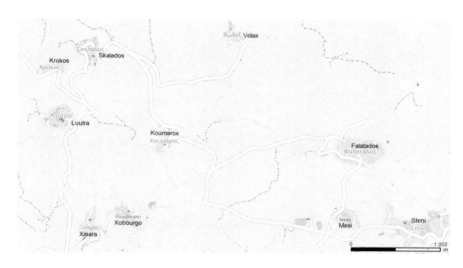

The trail Falatados - Volax

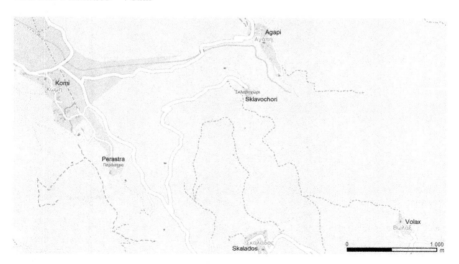

The trail Volax - Agapi

161

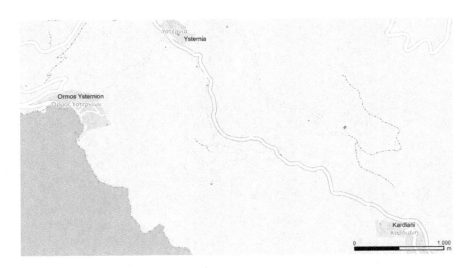

The trail Ormos Ysternion (Bight of Ysternia) - Ysternia

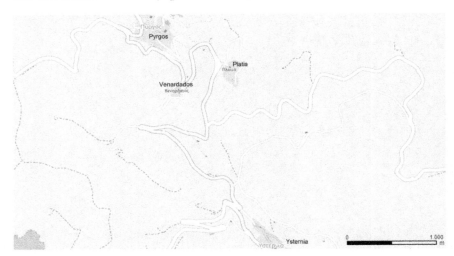

The trail Venardados – Pyrgos

162

Syros
The noble heart
of the Cyclades

Part I. Ano Syros
Eight centuries of history and culture overlook the Aegean sea

1. A rare cultural jewel

On arrival at the harbour of Hermoupolis, the image seen by the visitor is the most typical of Syros: a large city that spreads wide and climbs on two hills. On the top of each hill a large church: the Resurrection on the right and Saint George on the left.

These two hills symbolize the special cultural identity of Syros: the Resurrection is Orthodox, Saint George is Catholic and they represent the two religious communities that inhabit the island.

On arrival at Syros by boat: on the left the hill of San Tzortzis with the church of Saint George, on the right the hill of Anastasia with the church of the Resurrection

At first sight, they look like two hills of about the same height, where Hermoupolis has climbed. In fact, however, the left hill is much taller. It is just more to the rear and its height is not visible. And it is not Hermoupolis going up on it. It is a medieval fortified town, seven centuries older than Hermoupolis. And completely, but completely different.

In the foreground, the 19th-century neoclassical Hermoupolis, in the background the 13th-century medieval fortified town of Ano Syros

Hermoupolis is the largest neoclassical ensemble in Greece, founded only in 1822. It was once the largest city of the new Greek state, its largest port, and its cultural capital. On the other hand, Ano Syros is one of the best preserved medieval fortified towns of the Aegean, founded in the 13th century. And moreover, it is one of the few that are still inhabited. This further increases its importance. Which, in any case, is particularly great because of its historical and architectural value.

2. Historical peculiarities

In 1207, three years after the crusaders of the Fourth Crusade occupied the Byzantine Empire, Marco Sanudo, a Venetian aristocrat, and nephew of the doge Enrico Dandolo, occupied most of the Cycladic islands. He founded the Duchy of the Archipelago and settled in Naxos. This state included Syros. And then the cultural specificity of this island began being created…

When Greece was conquered by the crusaders, most of the inhabitants remained Orthodox. Catholicism was mostly represented by the feudal aristocracy of the conquerors. But Tinos and Syros are an exception to this rule. Here, the majority of the population embraced Catholicism. This was a long process that lasted throughout Venetian domination and continued during Ottoman domination after the conquest of the Cyclades by the Turks. This was practically done in 1537, with the attack of Hayreddin Barbarossa, the Ottoman Admiral-of-the-Fleet, and typically in 1566, when the last Duke of the Archipelago died. Then the islands officially joined the Ottoman Empire.

This historical development is reflected in the horizon of the fortified town through the monuments that stand out. Below the cathedral of Saint George, we see two historical monasteries: that of the Jesuits and that of the Capuchins. The dome of the former and the bell tower of the latter are typical landmarks in the outline of the hill of Ano Syros.

One would expect that these monasteries were founded during Venetian domination. And yet not. They were founded during Ottoman domination. The Venetians were always in great rivalry with the Pope and were not favourable to the strengthening of the Catholic Church in their lands. Therefore, they did not allow the establishment of Catholic monasteries. But when the Cyclades finally became Ottoman, in 1566, their Catholic populations were a good pretext for the French kings to intervene in the Ottoman Empire.

King Francis I had already signed a treaty in 1535 with Sultan Suleiman the Magnificent. According to it, all the Catholics of the empire would be under his protection. The French kings sent French monks and nuns who founded monasteries on many islands.

The Capuchins and Jesuits came to Syros in the 17th century. The Capuchins founded the monastery of Saint John in 1635, while the Jesuits settled permanently in Ano Syros and founded the monastery that includes the older church of Our Lady of Mount Carmel (1581) only in 1744. When France later changed its politics, the French were replaced by locals. They keep these institutions until today.

Some of them housed schools that later became so famous for offering good French education that they attracted students from as far as Madagascar, especially the Ursulines' schools in Naxos and Tinos. But originally they were the first schools on these islands since antiquity. Perhaps King Francis did not have the most unselfish motives, but we must admit that he offered a great service to the Cyclades and beyond.

The initial schools no longer exist. However, the educational tradition continues by the Brothers of the Christian Schools (known as Frères), who keep their schools a little farther, at the border with Hermoupolis.

The hill of Ano Syros, crowned by the cathedral of Saint George. A little below and on the right is the dome of Our Lady of Mount Carmel of the Jesuit monastery, and farther down and on the right, the bell tower of Saint John of the Capuchin monastery

3. Ano Syros and Hermoupolis

This French protection had a consequence of great historical significance for modern Greece: it became the cause of the creation of Hermoupolis, the urban, economic, industrial, and cultural centre of 19th-century Greece.

With the destruction of Chios by the Turks in 1822, during the Greek Revolution, many refugees came to Syros because, due to the old treaty that protected the areas with Catholic populations, the Turks could not harm them here.

They were followed by the inhabitants of the destroyed islands of Psara and Kasos in 1824 and many others from different regions of Greece and Asia Minor. All of them settled in the previously uninhabited port of Syros, under the medieval settlement, which until then was simply called Chora or Apano (upper) Chora.

So, until 1822, Ano Syros was the island's only settlement. Piracy that plagued the Aegean made the inhabitants gather at the top of the steep rock so that all together they would be able to cope better with them. The limited space resulting from this concentration forced the inhabitants to find solutions to create room for everyone. Thus, the houses were extended over the street and created the 'stegadia' or 'steadia', namely, the covered passageways, over which there are rooms of neighbouring houses.

4. Entering Ano Syros

Although it is impossible to get to Ano Syros without going through Hermoupolis, we will start from the former. Thus, you will visit the sights chronologically and understand them better.

Entering Ano Syros. One of the many 'stegadia', providing extra space from above. This was necessary in the confined space of a medieval settlement, where the houses were attached to one another in order to create a wall for protection against pirates

After entering Ano Syros, you will soon be on the main street, Piazza. Here are all the stores.

Piazza, the main street of Ano Syros

5. At the house of Markos Vamvakaris

And a surprise for many: walking into Ano Syros you will definitely stumble upon the house where its most famous child was born: the rebetiko's leading composer, Markos Vamvakaris. Today his home is a museum and you can visit it.

The house - museum of Markos Vamvakaris. The great composer of rebetiko was born here

The church of Saint Sebastian. The only parish church of this saint in Greece

Another one of the many 'stegadia', at the Capuchin monastery

6. The first historical monument:
The Capuchin monastery

The church of Saint John, of the Capuchin monastery. In its yard, the elders met during the Ottoman domination. The underground crypts of the church provided shelter during pirate raids

One of the rare cases where we see a sahnisin (wooden closed balcony) in a place where wood is scarce

photo by Denis Roubien

A typical particularly narrow 'stegadi'. The bell tower of the Capuchin monastery is visible behind it

A very rare case of a wooden and even elaborate shelter. Obviously a neoclassical
addition after Independence

A particularly impressive 'stegadi'

Traditional ceilings are covered with 'fides' (snakes), a local kind of cedar

The cathedral of Saint George

Ano Syros on the left and Hermoupolis on the right. View from the chapel of Kioura of Plaka

Kioura (Lady) of Plaka (1686). From here you will see the view to the rock of Ano Syros and Hermoupolis

photo by Denis Roubien

Climbing to Saint George from the back of the settlement. On the right, Saint Michael Taxiarchis

Saint George as seen looking from below

7. The next historical monument:
The Jesuit monastery

The church of Our Lady of Mount Carmel of the Jesuit monastery. It was built in 1581. The marble façade dates from 1824, which makes it one of the oldest marble constructions of such scale in modern Greece

8. The last and most impressive historical monument: The cathedral of Saint George

Cathedral of Saint George. It was rebuilt after many disasters in 1652. Its current form arose from the renovation of 1832-1834

At the top of the hill of San Tzortzis, you will see the trademark of the fortified town and the emblematic image of the island for centuries, when there was only Ano Syros. It is of great historical importance since it is the seat of the Catholic bishop, next to the building of the Catholic Diocese of Syros, where the island's oldest archives are preserved for centuries. But it was also the last stronghold against pirate raids since it is also the settlement's highest point.

The church of the Holy Trinity (1604)

The Holy Trinity again

9. Ano Syros today

Unfortunately, the change in the way of life has made the narrow streets of Ano Syros and its small houses unfit for the increased demands of today's humans. Result: from 6,000, which was the population of Ano Syros for centuries, now there are only a few hundred inhabitants. Most of them left for Athens or went down to Hermoupolis. However, the efforts to get Hermoupolis and Ano Syros to join UNESCO's World Heritage List are optimistic messages for the future.

For the moment, you make the effort to go up there, walk through its streets, visit its monuments and enjoy the view from the balconies of the restaurants and cafés. Looking at the sea, which no longer brings pirates, but visitors who are flocking more and more to this island of enormous cultural density.

Hermoupolis from the balconies of Ano Syros

Part II. Hermoupolis
The incarnation of the Greek miracle

1. A concentrated Greece

In the background, Ano Syros, crowned with the Catholic cathedral of Saint George, was the only settlement on the island until 1822. Hermoupolis was then created at its foot

The title of this chapter may seem exaggerated to you. However, you will change your mind if you learn the history of Hermoupolis. As we said, for centuries, Syros had only the medieval settlement of Ano Syros. The area underneath was empty, a wasteland, like the whole island.

Until 1822, when refugees fleeing the Turks who were destroying resurrected areas benefited from the island being protected by the kings of France and started settling in the wasteland.

The hill of Anastasia, with the Orthodox church of the Resurrection (Anastasis) as a 'counterweight' to the Catholic Saint George of Ano Syros

All these brought the knowledge and specialities for which their regions were distinguished. Thus, Hermoupolis became a kaleidoscope and a miniature of all Hellenism: a concentrated Greece, which gathered in a small space all the characteristics of the most distinguished Greeks, since the most creative and those who fought the most for their survival arrived here.

This is why Hermoupolis embodies the modern Greek miracle of survival and creativity. Within a few years, and for many decades afterwards, Hermoupolis became the largest city of the Greek state, which was created in the meantime. Moreover, it was a candidate for capital, and the main reason for its rejection was the absence of a hinterland on such a small island. But it was not just the largest city. Due to the special features of its settlers, it immediately became the largest commercial and cultural centre of Greece.

2. Miaouli Square. The former heart of Greece

Perhaps the most eloquent testimony of the greatness that Hermoupolis has known is its central square, former Otto Square, and today Miaouli Square. The buildings that surround it constitute one of Greece's most magnificent architectural ensembles. Suffice it to compare the Town Hall, the work of the German architect Ernst Ziller, with the Athens Town Hall, built at the same time, to understand the position of Hermoupolis in 19th-century Greece. It is the grandest town hall in the whole country (with its current limits) and one of its most impressive public buildings. And of course, like most of Hermoupolis, it is neoclassical.

When Greece became an independent State in 1830, classicism was introduced by the Bavarian King Otto, a fervent admirer of ancient Greece. However, it was observed more faithfully by the upper class, who wanted to be 'modern' and 'European'. The people stayed attached to traditional architecture, which better served their everyday needs, occasionally adding neoclassical details in order not to stay excluded from the revival of ancient culture in its birthplace, as they saw classicism at the time. Hermoupolis having been once the most important city in Greece, the 'official' classicism is more frequent here than in most other Greek cities, making Hermoupolis second only to Athens in that respect.

The town hall houses also the Archaeological Museum with very important findings, especially from Prehistory. The Cyclades occupied a prominent position in Prehistory, thanks to their central location in the Aegean Sea. The islands of the Aegean acted as a bridge uniting Europe to Asia and profited from the commercial activities between these lands, their ports receiving the ships which ensured that trade. The 3rd millennium BC, i.e. the Early Bronze Age, was the era of the so-called Cycladic civilization, which created the world-famous astonishing Cycladic figurines. These works of art in local white marble impress by their abstract forms, which inspired many modern artists. At that time the Cyclades had a dense population, installed in small settlements along the islands' coasts and Syros experienced particular prosperity.

However, the settlements of the Cycladic civilization had a violent end, which resulted in the interruption of this artistic creation. Around 2000 BC, the Cyclades started being influenced by the Minoan civilization of Crete, the new emerging power in the Aegean Sea. That led to a new period of prosperity in the Cyclades, which ended with the decline of Crete around 1500 BC and the arrival of the Mycenaeans, who dominated the last phase of the Bronze Age in Greece (Mycenaean period, 1600-1100 BC).

The two most important sites which gave most of the prehistoric findings are Kastri and Chalandriani, in the northern, almost uninhabited part of the island. Kastri is a settlement dating from 2800-2300 BC. Possibly, it was here that Syros was inhabited for the first time. South of Kastri is the small settlement of Chalandriani, where a prehistoric acropolis (fortress) has been excavated, as well as a large cemetery, from where most of the findings come.

The Geometric period (900-700 BC) followed the two centuries of chaos engendered by the arrival of the Dorians in about 1100 BC and the subsequent fall of the Mycenaean civilization. Syros is now mainly inhabited by Ionians who came from Attica.

In the Archaic period (7th – 6th century BC), which followed the Geometric period, some islands experienced a new era of prosperity, but Syros was a relatively poor island. In the Classical period, all the Cyclades declined with the rise of Athens in the 5th century BC and their compulsory adhesion to the Athenian Alliance, which transformed them into Athens's satellites.

Miaouli Square. The Town Hall (1875-1891)

To the left of the Town Hall. The Ladopoulos building (1870), housing the Historical Archives of Hermoupolis

To the right of the Town Hall. The 'Hellas' club, today the Cultural Centre of the municipality. It was designed by the Italian architect Pietro Sampo and built in 1862-1863

The music platform (another testimony of the high cultural level of Hermoupolis) in Miaouli Square and the statue of the homonymous admiral from Hydra

3. 'Apollo' Theatre. Testimony of a high culture

The other testimony of the greatness of Hermoupolis and its high cultural level is the 'Apollo' Theatre. It was designed by Pietro Sampo (like the 'Hellas' club) and built in 1862-1864. It was modelled on the famous Italian opera theatres, as opera was then at its zenith in Europe. Great names of the international artistic firmament appeared here.

Great personalities of art are depicted on the roof of the 'Apollo' Theatre

The environment of the 'Apollo' Theatre is worthy of it

4. Vaporia. The grandeur of the Greek navy

Moving beyond Miaouli Square, to the north, we reach Vaporia (ships). The name of this neighbourhood testifies to the occupation of its inhabitants: ship owners, who, of course, constituted an important component of that time's society, since the first settlers came from naval islands.

The church that dominates Vaporia is Saint Nicholas the Rich. It is called so as to stand out from Saint Nicholas the Poor of Ano Syros. The church of the ship owners' quarter could not, of course, have been devoted to another saint.

The dome of Saint Nicholas the Rich

The façade of Saint Nicholas the Rich

The mansions of Vaporia forming the sea front

A sample of Palladian style (from the great Renaissance architect Andrea Palladio, who became a pan-European model), perhaps unique in Greece

5. All Hermoupolis a unique neoclassical ensemble

But what is characteristic of Hermoupolis is that the sights are not limited to a small number of buildings. Here you will see the largest neoclassical ensemble in the world, a unique spectacle.

Above, Tsiropina Square, where we can find the Prefecture of the Cyclades (below)

photo by Denis Roubien

photo by Denis Roubien

6. The Virgin Mary of Psara. The boat church

If you leave the centre of Hermoupolis, to the south, in the opposite direction in relation to Vaporia, you will reach Psariana, the district of the refugees from Psara who arrived here in 1824. A monument you should not miss here is the church of the Assumption of the Virgin, known as the Virgin Mary of Psara (Panaghia Psarianon), built by the refugees in 1828-1829. It is a church probably unique in Greece.

The bell tower of the church of the Dormition of the Virgin Mary can be seen on the left

You may have heard that this church houses an icon, a work of El Greco. This icon is particularly valuable because it is one of his few surviving works dating from before leaving Greece, when he still painted according to the Byzantine tradition of the Cretan School. A very different style from the one he is world-famous for. But, apart from this treasure, this church also hides others, unique in Greece.

The last time I found myself at Syros was during a conference. At the intervals, I engaged myself in systematically taking photos of the neoclassical houses, something I had not been able to do before. For five days I was taking photos for hours, covering the entire complex of Hermoupolis and Ano Syros. During my wanderings, I found the Virgin

Mary of Psara. Knowing that there, is the icon of El Greco, I went in to see it.

The icon is in the narthex, so after having seen it, I proceeded to the nave. Then I went out without observing anything special because I did not look above the door. Also, I did not meet anyone. That was important.

The Dormition of the Virgin, by El Greco. Church of the Virgin Mary of Psara (public domain work, {{PD-1923}})

Shortly before the ship's departure, one last walk and one last look at El Greco's icon. If you consider how scarce his works are in Greece (less than ten), you will understand why I went back there (it is not close, it is on the other side of the city centre). This time, however, the church was not empty.

There was Father Konstantinos, the vicar, who excitedly related the accidental discovery of the icon in 1983, under layers of varnish that made it seem an ordinary icon with no particular value. The discovery was due to the observation of an archaeologist, who suspected what was hidden beneath the varnish. Father Konstantinos, already then the church's vicar, was present at the event and even after all these years he will narrate to you the discovery with great emotion. But there is also something else he will tell you and show you with enthusiasm.

As Father Konstantinos will explain to you, since the inhabitants of Psara were famous sailors, their technical knowledge was much better in the construction of ships rather than buildings. The buildings of Psara were simple and humble. Their ships, however, were proportional to the island's great naval power.

So, Father Konstantinos will reveal to your stunned eyes a church that was built as a boat. First, he will show you the gallery. Instead of the familiar balcony with bars, you will see the stern of a ship, only instead of a mermaid, it has God the Father painted in its centre! This is what I had not noticed coming out of the church last time.

The gallery, in the form of the stern of a ship

The pulpit is of similar construction, although less apparent. But you will not find the boat only at the gallery and the pulpit. If you are not afraid of heights and precarious creaking wooden ladders, the agile Father Konstantinos will run up the scary rickety staircase to the interior of the roof, prompting you to follow him. Although he is over sixty, prepare for a run to catch up with him. When at last you will manage to reach the top of

231

the ladder and look through, over the roof of the interior of the church, you will not believe your eyes.

You will see a whole hull of a boat, overturned. This was the most robust wooden structure the people from Psara knew how to make and this is what they did. Do not forget that we are talking about a time when it was difficult to build a large church with a wooden roof and no dome.

The ceiling is in form of an overturned hull of a boat

In Greece, such roofs were unknown. In Hermoupolis, you will see the only example I know (and even that I did not know) so far. Who could believe that Syros, overloaded with treasures, has still more treasures to reveal? After five days of wandering, just one last walk before boarding revealed new treasures. So, wander as much as you can, look around and talk with those who are willing to talk to you. You may run into wonderful people who will reveal wonderful things to you.

The pulpit

7. Remnants of the industrial past

Going farther south, after Psariana, you will meet an impressive array of industrial buildings of a spectacular scale in relation to the island's size. Undeniable witnesses to the great industrial development that Syros has known, they are now dilapidated, testifying to the decline that followed when Piraeus became the main port of Greece. Some have found a new use, such as the Industrial Museum. Others patiently wait to be given a new destination, which will save them from abandonment and decay.

8. The resting place. Even here Hermoupolis stands out

On the same side of the city, another witness to the wealth that Hermoupolis experienced in the 19th century is also the resting place of its inhabitants. There are two cemeteries, the Orthodox and the Catholic ones. Since the Orthodox population included all ship owners and rich merchants, the Orthodox cemetery is the one that contains the most impressive burial monuments. Here, the sculptors of Tinos, the centre of marble craftsmanship of modern Greece, had the opportunity of creating many of the works that make them worthy heirs of Phidias.

To understand what cultural wealth we are talking about, think that the photos you see are a small selection. Only an on-site visit will give you the full picture of this modern Greek miracle called Hermoupolis.

photo by Denis Roubien

photo by Denis Roubien

242

243

photo by Denis Roubien

245

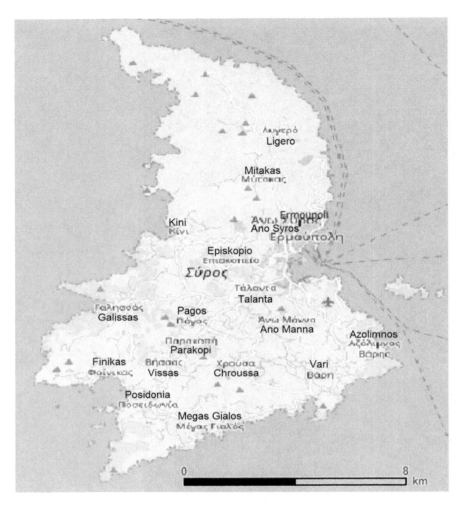

Map of Syros

About the author

Denis Roubien holds a PhD in Architectural History and is a professor in Higher Education and a fervent cultural hiker. The hiking trips in which he participates, along with other travel experiences, are recorded in his books.

Thank you for reading this book. If you have the time, a review would be very helpful.

Printed in Great Britain
by Amazon

24836355R00145